Know Your Judas

Know Your Judas

Machael LaShaunda

J. Kenkade
PUBLISHING®
Little Rock, Arkansas

Know Your Judas
Copyright © 2020 by Machael LaShaunda

All rights reserved. No part of this book may be photocopied, reproduced, distributed, uploaded, or transmitted in any form or by any means, or stored in a database or retrieval system, without the prior written permission of the publisher.

J. Kenkade Publishing
6104 Forbing Rd
Little Rock, AR 72209
www.jkenkadepublishing.com
Facebook.com/jkenkadepublishing

J. Kenkade Publishing is a registered trademark.

Printed in the United States of America
ISBN 978-1-944486-89-1

Scripture quotations marked NIV are taken from The Holy Bible, New International Version NIV Copyright© 1973, 1978, 1984, 2011 by Biblica, Inc. Used by permission. All rights reserved worldwide.

The views expressed in this book are those of the author and do not necessarily reflect the views of Publisher.

Table of Contents

Introduction	9
Judas of Disease	13
Judas of Discomfort	25
Judas of Discouragement	39
Judas of Disobedience	47
Judas of Distraction	57
Judas of Destruction	63
Judas of Disgrace	69
Judas of Distrust	75
Judas of Discord	79
Judas of Difficulty and Distress	85
Judas to be Revealed	91
References	95
About the Author	97
About J. Kenkade Publishing	99

"As you draw closer to your destiny, opposition will always become more fierce. The most dangerous being opposition from within your own camp. Don't be naïve to think that this will not be the case with you. Instead of thinking you don't or will not have a Judas in our life, you need to learn to deal with him/her." [1]

Introduction: Beneath the Veil

Throughout life, we'll always be confronted with difficulty, but one must become adept at learning how to name it, include it, and elevate from it. If you grew up in the church like me, hearing Judas' name may bring about adverse thoughts, emotions, or disappointment because of what we learned about him. Judas Iscariot is best known for betraying Jesus[2] and receiving payment from Jesus' enemies for the betrayal.[3] However, growing up, I didn't learn Judas was remorseful for his betrayal and confessed his sins.[3] Though not directly to Jesus, he tried to return the money to His enemies.[3] When rejected, Judas hung himself.[3] From a progressive viewpoint, Judas helped fulfill one of Jesus' purposes.

Judas, one of Jesus' original twelve apostles[4], betrayed his friend, teacher, and leader in the Garden of Gethsemane with a kiss[5] to make it clear to the authorities who they should arrest.[5] For three years, Judas had walked with Jesus. He received spiritual gifts to preach, heal, and cure diseases and had power and authority over all demons.[6] However, he harbored unconfessed sins, including deceit,[7] stealing,[7] and betrayal.[2] Since Judas stayed silent, Satan continued dividing him and Jesus.

You're probably wondering, if Judas did all of those things, how I could convince you that his purpose was remotely a good thing. Furthermore, if he didn't repent to Jesus, how did he try to make amends? Honestly, I'm not going to convince you his purpose was a good thing. In my opinion, a friend betraying a friend is never a good thing. However, if you think about some friendships you've lost due to betrayal, was the ended friendship a blessing in disguise?

It doesn't matter how it ended. Bottom line: was it for the better?

Be honest. How often do you apologize to someone you've knowingly offended? Did it take away the fact that you were remorseful and felt bad because of the things that transpired? Probably not because your heart was different in that moment. Like Judas.

I ponder the story of Judas.

The times I've thought or uttered the phrase "why me?" aloud are countless because I felt an injustice happening to me. Often, when I asked Jesus, "Why me?", it was disingenuous. I was simply complaining to Him about my problems, issues, and tribulations. I didn't realize it was something more until after I was done fussing and griping. Only then could God with His sweet spirit in a sweet voice say, "Know your Judas."

Oh my gosh!

That was a revelation for me. I was excited and relieved.

Now, my insight is different with only three words: "Know your Judas."

Sometime later, I knew this was to become a book. My book. A foundation for my story. I studied Judas' story more in depth. One thing I realized about Jesus' handling of Judas is that He hurried him only at the time of the betrayal, not because He had the inside scoop on Judas. You all know how we do when we find out someone is plotting or has plotted against us. Remember, Jesus gave Judas the same power and authority as the other apostles all while knowing what was to come. Judas had seen Jesus work first-hand. Jesus didn't dismiss Judas to be rude or exclude him from the other apostles out of frustration or anger or because He was finished with him. It was so that purpose would no longer be prolonged.

Let's pause. Jesus wasn't the only one with a Judas.

Moses had Pharaoh. David had Saul. Samson had Delilah. Naomi had grief. Esther had Hamon. The woman with the issue of blood had her ailment. These were all Judases. The list continues with you, family, friends, enemies, frenemies, and me, too. No one's exempt from trials, tribulations, or what in this book I'll name a Judas. For some of us, there are Judases because, let's be honest, we can be hit separately or simultaneously. To anyone who hasn't had a Judas, I will just say keep living. It's on the way. As you read through the pages of this book, I want you to be able to decipher your Judases so the purpose God has destined for you is fulfilled and is no longer prolonged.

Judas of Disease
✝

On my thirty-eighth birthday, I was restless and feeling emotional. At the stroke of midnight, tears flowed down my cheeks as I watched my husband sleep peacefully.

I whispered to myself, "Thank You, Lord, for another year."

Finally, after another hour or so of reflecting over my life, the blessings God gave me, and knowing I'm a miracle, I fell asleep. When I woke up, I wasn't feeling well. I wanted to pop out of bed, but my body didn't move quite how my mind envisioned. I was tired, but it was all right because overall things seemed to be going well. My vacation was in a couple of weeks, and I was determined to make it a wonderful day since God saw fit to let me live. Unfortunately, it was a facade created so I wouldn't have to face the truth.

Things are never that simple for me. In fact, I knew Judas was near.

Though I didn't want it to be, I knew this Judas was coming like a hurricane. If there's one thing I've learned about this Judas, it comes hard or not at all. During my Myasthenia Gravis (MG) flares, I pray, click my heels, and wish for the best of luck. Seriously, I must pray until the windows of Heaven open and every angel comes and sits with me.

I knew I was under duress, so I lay in bed a few extra minutes and repeated to myself quietly, "Today is not the day. I will be great."

While psyching myself up, I heard a sweet, deep voice say, "Happy birthday, baby."

As I lay with my back to this beautiful voice, I exhaled deeply and responded, trying to withhold the anger, tears, and grief I felt. "Thank you."

I mustered all the energy I could to sit up on my side to better situate myself for an easier transition of getting out of bed safely. Breathing heavier than normal and praying that Judas wasn't making a special guest appearance, I walked slowly to my bathroom. It was like walking the Green Mile. Those were the longest eighteen steps I've ever walked that morning. I wasn't prepared for what was about to be revealed.

I entered the bathroom, standing and staring at my reflection in the mirror. I discovered that the Judas of Disease came and betrayed me with a kiss while I slept. Once again, it returned strong, invading my space. One of my eyes was wide open, and the other eye was closed shut as if it were super glued. Now, every day, my eyes look sleepy. Usually, I hear all types of comments from people and tolerate them because their comments are stereotypical and characteristically birthed from ignorance. When my eyes started doing their own thing like a toddler who's decided no rules apply to them, I was frustrated because this was my first physical tell, a sign this wasn't ending well. People would know I wasn't well. That's not the attention I wanted, especially on my birthday.

Let me tell you, I was furious. I'm not going to pretend as if I weren't. I kept thinking, How in the entire world and why of all days would my MG flare up today?

After a short period of sulking in self-pity, I came to myself and realized that this wasn't something I hadn't met before. Therefore, I told myself, like the James Cleveland song says, "This, too, will pass."[8] Nevertheless, it didn't mean I wasn't disappointed for looking abnormal from what I was used to.

As I was silently crying in the bathroom, the same voice who'd wished me happy birthday before asked, "What's wrong?"

I couldn't respond without the frog in my throat leaping. I returned to the bedroom as if I were giving a great reveal. He saw my altered appearance. Without hesitation, he got out of the bed and hugged me tight, as if it would be his last time. I guess it was the sorrow and apprehension he had seen on my face.

As he hugged me, he whispered, "You're so beautiful to me. It's going to be okay, babe."

Tears continued streaming down my cheeks. He released me and looked in my eyes. He asked, "Do you need to stay home and get some rest?"

I sighed in relief and thought, God, thank You for this man.

I leaned in and continued crying as I shook my head no. Again, darkness came across my mind. "I hate Myasthenia." Between the pressures of work, home, family, church, life, and now the added foolery of MG on my birthday of all days, all I could do was cry out, "Baby Jesus, be a fence!"

I was over it, and my day had barely started. I felt like I was running out of options. I didn't know what else to do. I was following my neurologist's and therapist's orders. I was doing everything I could physically, spiritually, emotionally, and financially at home, work, and church. Honestly, I was overextended. It seemed like I couldn't catch a break, but I'm not the girl to say no.

"Help me, baby Jesus. What am I doing wrong?"

I've asked God this question so many times

before, but I had to ask Him again. I felt ignored because I didn't think He was listening. He wasn't responding to me, at least not with the response I wanted. Truthfully, when I was asking for help, my terms were conditional and not what was best for me.

Remember, my husband asked if I needed to stay home and rest, but I responded with "No! Ah! What is wrong with me?"

I knew where this was headed. I'd named my Judas, and I personally know the capabilities of the Judas of Disease. MG is more than making my eyes do something out of the ordinary. Still, it didn't stop me from feeling abandoned and being stubborn.

"Hello?! Can You hear me?"

I felt alone. My stress continued to rise. Things were spiraling out of control rapidly, and I couldn't understand why. Then again, was it that I didn't want to understand or accept the why?

"Not today, Jesus. Please!" I pleaded repeatedly with Him, but it didn't matter because my eyes kept getting worse as I continued begging Him to take it away. He wouldn't. It stayed like an unwanted houseguest.

"Oh my gosh, seriously?"

I kept looking in the mirror every five minutes to see if it was gone like an in-between-blessings person checking their bank account to see if their check has hit their account yet.

It's me. I'm the in-between-blessings person. There were only two things left for me to do. Since I'd already prayed, I clicked those heels and wished for the best of luck because the day would go on.

"Hello, Judas of Disease, it's time for work."

I went to work and then out to eat afterwards with friends and family to celebrate my birthday– tired, ill and all, but I refused to let MG win. I was so determined to overcome, I worked until my vacation. I called and messaged my doctor about my symptoms. He wanted to see me, but I refused to go into the office because I knew that was going to mess up my vacation plans. Instead of embracing my Judas, things got worse. Even on vacation. I was on a cruise. This meant I couldn't visit my neurologist or be rushed to the hospital if I needed emergency medical treatment. Besides, I needed treatment far beyond my eyes. I was delusional thinking it was going to fix itself. This flare up had passed go and collected two hundred dollars at least three times. Nonetheless, I was so caught up in doing things my own way, trying to fight this Judas the wrong way, now my "Help me, baby Jesus. Jesus, be a fence" prayer was much different. I paid tremendously for it, too.

I mentioned MG could be a hurricane. Well, it was more like a tsunami when it finished with me. No mercy. At least, it seemed merciless. Reflecting now, there was a lot of mercy. In the beginning, I didn't do like Jesus and tell my Judas of Disease, "What you are about to do, do it quickly."[9]

I tried to rebuke it and pray it away, and when those didn't work, I simply tried to ignore it. However, this Judas wouldn't leave until it was given permission to fulfill its purpose. Once I gave the Judas of Disease the permission to do it quickly, the purpose was fulfilled.

Though my disease probably isn't your disease, think about how many times you've tried to pray away, rebuke away, or ignore something that was meant to serve a purpose in your life. Instead of embracing your Judas to have the purpose fulfilled sooner rather than later, you found yourself going through a whirlwind of circumstances because you weren't ready to surrender your power.

That was me. Having had MG nearly all my life, I know a lot of ins and outs of this disease. Subconsciously, I knew what I was doing was only to my downfall. I was like Peter when he tried to protect Jesus from being arrested.[10] He was trying to prevent something he didn't realize was already set in motion. I was doing the same thing, ignoring what was already set in motion to manifest. However, Jesus stopped Peter[10] from making a grave mistake that could have altered our reality.

If he hadn't, we wouldn't be singing Margaret Pleasant Douroux's "If it had not been for the

Lord on my side, tell me where would I be, where would I be?"[11] Instead, we'd be singing, "Would we be" if Peter had had his way that night.

I'm not that person anymore. When it comes to my MG, I take it seriously. Understand, I know my disease is serious. However, there is a difference between knowing something is serious and taking it seriously. Because I've had MG forever, unconsciously I was taking it for granted. I'd gotten used to living my "normal". I'd become so good at getting it stable before any real damage could be done, I wasn't paying enough attention to notice that God was trying to get my attention. I was focused on the natural when, in fact, it was something more. I was on a path to be reconnected spiritually through a physical ailment. If it weren't for a spiritual reconnection, what other reason would God send the Judas of Disease?

God knew the only way I'd take a break or relax was by force. By any means necessary, He had to do what needed to be done because it would be the only way I'd be still. I'm not saying this was one of my fondest moments, but purpose was fulfilled. During this time, I reconnected with things I'd lost over the years: "love, joy, peace, forbearance, kindness, goodness, faithfulness, gentleness, and self-control."[12] I restored relationships and relearned who I am. I'm still reconnecting with that girl. What God was giving me wasn't well-received because of its packaging yet, despite my tantrum, He still saw fit for me to learn the lesson.

I don't know your story, and I don't have to know it. However, I know we've all been reluctant to accept help when we needed it during our times of disease, possibly because we don't want people in our business, we're headstrong and independent, or we're hung up on ourselves.

Let me be the first – or second, third, fourth, or fifth – to tell you that it's great to be something to someone. It's an incredible feeling knowing you're the rock everyone counts on… until you've emptied yourself of all you have because you've been the something and rock to everyone but haven't stopped to be replenished. What was once great becomes a chore.

No matter your disease– stress, insecurity, depression, divorce, financial difficulty, unemployment, mental illness, autoimmune disorder, diabetes, cancer, iron deficiency, heart problems, high blood pressure, low self-esteem, fear, alcoholism, drug abuse, or sex abuse, and so on– self-care is vital.

Take a moment to be replenished so you can continue being great.

Don't be who I was, feeling bad if I had to take a break because I wanted people to believe my health was stable and trying to prove to myself that I had control of MG and it didn't have control of me.

Sadly, in that moment and others like it, I failed. Catastrophically.

There have been times I've won against the Judas of Disease. However, those don't matter because this time I lost to my Judas of Disease the hard way. A weeklong stay in the ICU, nasogastric tube, aggressive intravenous infusion treatments, and extensive and intense respiratory, occupational, physical, and speech therapies had to take place so that the Judas of Disease's purpose could be fulfilled. My muscles weren't the only things on a fast decline. I was put on FMLA and given three new prescriptions for migraines, nausea, and lack of rest.

Though resting was hard, in time, I learned how to do it successfully. In my most vulnerable moment, people I knew and those I didn't know were showing up in many ways for my family and me. It was God showing me that when I felt alone, abandoned, unloved, and so many other emotions, He had people who kept me in their hearts and on their minds. When I felt like I was about to lose everything in my life, God showed me I wasn't the only one He allowed to give to freely and offer some healing and encouragement. He reminded me that though I was indirectly praying to have this cup passed from me[5], it wasn't His will...yet. He had something greater for me.

I've accepted MG.

I'm more open about it and my journey with it. I try to encourage others as much as I can, including other "snowflakes" (MG patients).

I've learned it's nice to be nice.

It costs nothing to give an encouraging word, hug, or smile. I want to say to you: don't fight against your disease. Also, don't become so content with it that you're taking advantage of it and ignoring signs that your mind and body give you to do something different. The Judas of Disease comes in many forms, but the common denominator is that self-care is the best medicine. According to Dictionary.com, self-care is "the act of attending to one's physical or mental health, generally without medical or other professional consultation. The products or practices used to comfort or soothe oneself".[13]

Don't mistake my acceptance of MG as an indication that I've succumbed or surrendered to it. It's quite the opposite. It simply means I've learned how to battle my disease in a healthy way. I've learned my power isn't proving to people that I'm a robot. Instead, it's revealing I'm human. With error. I'm not fail-proof but instead someone who wants to live to see her grandchildren, great-grandchildren and great-great-grandchildren and do well by the legacy I've been fortunate to build because of my ancestors before me.

If for any reason you're feeling inadequate because you have a disease, I want you to know that you're not inadequate. You are going to be exactly who and what God has destined you to be. You have purpose. So, look your Judas of Disease in the face and tell it, "What you are about to do, do it quickly[8] because I have purpose to fulfill."

Judas of Discomfort
✝

I wish I could tell you that I lived a normal life, had a normal childhood, or that all my dreams came true, but I can't. Why wasn't my life normal, you ask? Why didn't I have a normal childhood? Why haven't all my dream come true? I was a toddler when my parents received the news that I had Myasthenia Gravis, a rare, incurable autoimmune neuromuscular disease that attacks all voluntary muscles. MG symptoms differ in each patient, which sometimes makes it difficult to diagnose. Ironically, because my eyes were droopy, I was diagnosed sooner than patients who may not show any physical signs.

Now, let me paint the picture for you. If you're a parent, you're probably feeling some sort of empathy. If you're familiar with autoimmune diseases, you have an idea about the struggles I combat daily. Before I continue, let me say that I'm not telling you this for empathy, sympathy, or compassion.

This is to help you name your Judas.

Imagine you're a parent of a toddler with underdeveloped speech. Initially, you believe it's because she's a toddler. However, when you add MG, it's clear she can't communicate adequately because her throat muscles are too weak. Furthermore, she can't communicate when her throat muscles are too weak to eat or drink, which becomes a major safety hazard because she can choke on anything she has to swallow, including her saliva. Added to that, when her leg muscles are too weak, she stumbles and falls for what seems to be no obvious reason. Simultaneously, her eyesight is either double or blurry, so she walks into walls, doors, and other objects. MG is a disease that debilitates the body, causing severe weakness or temporary paralysis. This is no one's fault, but that doesn't mean it's not uncomfortable seeing your child experience this or that you won't feel like you did something wrong during the pregnancy or failed as a parent because you can't change this new reality for your child and family. Instead, you're obligated to embrace this unwanted company forcing itself into your life.

There are parents who have watched more doctors than they could count poke and prod their child. They observe doctors running countless tests searching for a positive diagnosis because the standard tests they ran were negative. These same parents meet with too many doctors to even remember all of their names or those who practice in areas of expertise that require a referral from a primary care physician. These parents have had to learn what ailment was attacking their child, how to pronounce it, what to research, and everything they could about this disease, including which doctors could treat their child. This isn't something any parent prepares for, especially not those who have had normal and successful pregnancies previously. This was something unprecedented for my family.

However, MG wasn't the only ailment that forced my family to adjust. At that time, my family's greatest concern was that I wouldn't live through my adolescent years. According to the doctors, if I did, I'd be dependent on my parents and family because I'd never live a normal life, unable to care for myself. Not to mention, doctors had limited information and resources for this disease.

The fact is my God had something else in mind for me.

While still trying to adjust to MG, my family was met with another ailment a few years later. My father suddenly died after suffering a stroke exactly one week after my sixth birthday. Doctors told my mom he died peacefully in his sleep.

Let's backtrack. My father was in the hospital recovering from a heart attack he'd suffered before the stroke. It was a Sunday after he'd preached at church. I remember staying home with my mom, and my siblings had to go to church with my dad. Since I'm a daddy's girl, there was a heated discussion, and we went a few rounds about whether I would go with my dad or stay home with my mom. Soon, that would be irrelevant when that phone call came, and my mom heard what no one wants to hear – that her husband was being rushed to the hospital. The details she gathered were that he had complained of chest pain and he left out of the sanctuary after preaching what may have been his best sermon. It was possible he had a heart attack.

I was young, and I watched my mom on the phone, listening as she received and gave out important information. We had a rotary phone. What was supposed to be a mommy and daughter day became the day our lives changed forever.

I'm a true daddy's girl, even in spirit.

I talk to him often and think of him even more. Though I was young when he died, I have memories of him. They are few, but they are very fond to me.

Let's recap. I have a rare muscle disease, and now my dad was in the hospital fighting for his life. This Judas was not playing around. It was like a Big Mama giving out whoopings because the kids didn't listen, and she was fed up.

No questions asked. No explanations needed. Only repercussions.

I don't remember when he went into the hospital or how many days he was there, but the last time I saw my dad alive was that Sunday morning when he kissed me and Mom goodbye. Little did I know, that would be the last kiss I'd receive from him or words I'd hear him speak to me. Back in those days, children weren't allowed in patients' rooms. This was particularly hard because my dad and I couldn't see each other for my birthday. In fact, I spent that birthday at the hospital. Thinking about it in retrospect, knowing my father went into the hospital but didn't come back home may be a reason I'm not a fan of them. It's almost like a fear. I was taught that doctors help you. I was taught that the hospital is where you go to get better so you can be with your family. However, the first formed memory of a hospital I have isn't what I was told but what I had experienced.

I have dreams that will forever be pending because I know they will never happen on this side of Heaven, dreams like my dad seeing me graduate beyond preschool, get married, have children, or write and publish this book. There are various accomplishments, mistakes, and milestones I've had without him, and I can't tell stories to my children and husband because our relationship was cut short. Instead, I wonder a lot. I let my mind wander and entertain thoughts of "what if...?" and "If my daddy were alive..."

It's impossible because, on this side, death is forever. A part of me wanted my dad to be a Lazarus. I cried and yelled at God so many times about my dad's death and how it made me feel, but no matter how many tears I cried or how loud I shouted, it was evident my dad wasn't Lazarus. His destiny wasn't to rise on this side.

My father's death is still a struggle for me. In a way, I feel cheated. It wasn't his choice to leave his family. He had greater purpose to fulfill beyond this realm because his work was finished on this side. I can't explain how I felt when I finally understood my father's death. For years, I constantly asked what happened to him. It became insufferable for my siblings to visit his gravesite or listen to my mom explain to me repeatedly until it resonated. Despite the fact that I stopped asking, I didn't understand. I only recognized the hurt my family experienced each time I asked that question. Frankly, I don't know if I didn't understand because I was young or if I simply didn't want to accept my dad's death. Whatever it was, my mind wouldn't process the new reality my family was thrust into. In my opinion, this was worse than the news of my MG diagnosis. Of course, I'm biased because I wasn't my caretaker. Despite everything, as I got older, I understood this altered, harsh reality because I watched my dreams slowly fade.

In essence, I haven't accepted this reality. I've just adapted and lived with it.

As a result, I was introduced to my next Judas, one many of us know intimately: the Judas of Discomfort.

Everyone has been dealt a hard hand – or two, three, four, or five hands – before. I don't expect my life to be different. However, what separates me is my outlook. The Judas of Discomfort came into my family's home like a flood and seemed to do a lot of long-term damage because we weren't prepared to handle the aftershock. The Judas of Disease also came and stayed because depression, self-pity, and so many other uneasy feelings were existent during that time. What was once a happy home was soon filled with grief, heartache, and shattered spirits. As my family was managing and adjusting to our new reality, I didn't know these spirits and emotions were functioning.

Life continuously shifted. When my dad passed, we moved. I didn't want to because I thought if we moved, he wouldn't be able to find us at our new home. Things seemed out of control because everything happening around me was uncontrollable. I had six years in a home that made life feel unwavering and coherent, and now everything was unbalanced and so uncomfortable.

In the interest of transparency, I'll tell you that this chapter is a bit hard for me because of some of the things I'm forcing myself to admit...to myself. It's difficult to think that I've suppressed a great deal of feelings just to survive or for the sake of comfort. Discomfort at times seem unbearable.

The Judas of Discomfort did a number on that six-year-old girl. She's not six anymore. Here and now, she understands she has purpose. For that reason, Judas of Discomfort, I release you to go and do it quickly.

My story isn't your story. My testimony isn't your testimony. However, if you've decided to look your Judas of Discomfort in the face and release it to fulfill its purpose in your life, then you know this is only part of the process to get the growth desired out of you.

"Embrace the process to see the progress" is an expression I created. I'll say this, even though I don't always want to face discomfort directly, I know blessings I've been praying and asking God for won't come if I'm not willing to grow through some discomforts to receive them.

Contemplate this. A woman with a typical successful pregnancy will endure three trimesters before giving birth, and mothers take measures to know what's coming with each stage of pregnancy. Each trimester is different. Experts say the first trimester is the most crucial for the mom-to-be.[14] While the pregnancy experience is different for each mom, each pregnancy goes through transformation so the baby can live outside of the mother's womb. Her body expands so the baby can grow during the gestation stage. The mom-to-be makes necessary adjustments for the baby's healthy development, including ceasing any unhealthy practices or risky habits, attending regular doctor visits, eating a healthy diet, and so on. The trimesters may cause some discomfort. However, the mom-to-be understands that what's coming after the gestation stage is worth the temporary discomfort. High-risk mothers who have tighter restrictions will also endure discomfort to ensure a successful and safe delivery of their baby. This is growth.

A mom-to-be knows before anyone else that they're expecting. Therefore, she begins making lifestyle changes to ensure her baby will be healthy and safe because development is crucial. A loving and caring mom will make up her mind to protect her baby, even in the womb.

I believe that when God allows us to encounter the Judas of Discomfort, it's to prune us and not punish us because in our next level of elevation, some things attached to us that survived where we are currently won't survive our next level. This doesn't mean the things God is pruning aren't good for us. It just means, in the climate we're advancing to, those things are unnecessary and won't survive. The chances of survival for a baby born prematurely may not be good. Therefore, the closer the mom-to-be carries her baby to full-term, the higher the survival rate.

After birth, some things the baby needed during the gestation stage aren't needed anymore. They're pruned away. Otherwise, they become dead weight. The pruning might be painful and uncomfortable. During the labor, it may seem like so many things are happening simultaneously, but the mom-to-be remembers something great is coming from this. Therefore, she pushes through being in a temporary state of discomfort. You, too, must push through.

I experienced discomfort when my father died. I didn't know I'd experience this same discomfort repeatedly over the next three decades, losing close relatives and a childhood friend. Finally, when I was able to get on the healing path, the Judas of Discomfort returned like a plague. Now I'm coping with the loss of eight relatives, six who were immediate, in a twelve-month time frame. After a few decades of losses and then the one-year equivalent of those losses, I'm just enduring this discomfort. I won't lie. I'm struggling with this Judas because the grief is devastating. Nevertheless, I won't fret because God does this same process to spiritually grow us. Each elevation comes with some discomfort. Certain Judases of Discomfort may come sporadically, while others come simultaneously. Some discomforts may be more uncomfortable than others because of the gift or purpose coming from them. This go-around, the Judas of Discomfort hit my family simultaneously, swift and severe. Along with the losses, other family members also sustained life-threatening health challenges. A couple of those challenges were things my dad succumbed to. However, in this season, I understand God is pruning us. As each day passes, I receive a better understanding about why it all had to happen.

I have some resentment because I should've written and published a book years ago. My "dreams come true" pending list keeps growing. However, a lot has changed from then to now after taking all those "L's", including my faith, hope, and trust in God. Our relationship is amazing.

It's easy for me to explain. I quit thinking about memories I can never create with those who are gone. Instead, I focus on who God kept here to go with me to my next level. I'm blessed. We're all blessed. When we make the conscious decision to give our Judas of Discomfort permission to work freely, God can begin His pruning process in our lives so we can be promoted to the next level.

It would be a bold-faced lie if I told you I don't miss my family members who have gone on. However, with a pure heart, I can say if it hadn't happened, I wouldn't be who I am in this very moment. Therefore, I reconcile my grief with knowing while they were here, they gave me all they could. I'm blessed with longevity and a strong foundation in my faith. Now, I must take what I've learned and pass it on to other generations.

For that reason, Judas of Discomfort, bring it because I'm at the place in my life where I understand it had to happen. Though I'm not okay yet, one day I will be. For that, it's okay.

If there are things you're going through or have come through in your life and they made you uncomfortable, so uncomfortable that it was hard to face or speak about, ask yourself this question: how many times has something gone away because you didn't face it or because it made you uncomfortable? If your answer is "never", then you know trouble isn't biased. It is no respecter of persons. Discomfort lingers with a foul aroma, filling the room until it has been released from its space.

Have you ever entered a space, possibly a home, car, restroom, kitchen, outdoors, etc., and there was a stale or foul smell? Although you were uncomfortable because your sense of smell was heightened to this unpleasant odor, you also noticed others were content. Maybe you were the only one who smelled it. The others possibly became comfortable with the foul smell. Perhaps they became complacent or used to it. It could've been that their sense of smell wasn't as heightened as yours. Nevertheless, you stayed quiet, though you were uncomfortable. Therefore, your disposition and demeanor changed.

The Judas of Discomfort often does this to us. It lingers. You know it's there, but you avoid saying or doing anything to add to the discomfort. After a while of avoidance, you become complacent to the discomfort like the others around you, and without notice but with silent consent, you've taken on the attitude of "it is what it is".

Avoiding discomfort causes more than complacency. It allows discomfort to fester. It builds up a toxic immune system. What shouldn't be allowed or accepted as normalcy becomes a part of your habits, routines, and– ultimately– your lifestyle.

Judas of Discomfort. The silent one.

I won't tell you how to handle your Judas, but I'll say that not handling it has never worked out for the better or produced the growth needed for us to function in our next season of promotion.

Judas of Discouragement
†

2019 beat me down. Literally. It shattered my soul from a place I only thought existed in theory. The year was a blur. Dreadful. Just sad.

2020 didn't get better. In fact, it got worse. To be fair, the entire world suffered in 2020. I get a smidge depressed just thinking about 2019 and 2020. Of course, throughout these years, there have been a few admirable, memorable moments. Happy times. Celebratory occasions.

However, ask me to sum up my 2019-2020 experience in one sentence, and I'd say, "This content is unavailable." That's how merciless and ruthless I felt it was to my family and me. I'm still speechless. At one point, I said, "If someone would've told me the price of 2019 and 2020, I would've said, 'Hard pass!'" My sentiment: just throw both years out with the trash.

I wanted to quit. I felt dejected, uninspired, alone, shattered, destroyed, weary, defeated, heartbroken, distressed, and in a rut.

You name it, I felt it.

That's right. The Judas of Discouragement found my address, my house became an Airbnb, and it overstayed its unwelcome. Nearly every month, something happened, whether it was my health or someone in my family's health, financial hardships, mental and emotional breakdowns, physical impairments, unemployment, or death.

I'm a faith believer, but life had gotten a tight grip on me. My emotions had nothing to do with it. These were solely life's reoccurrences, and I felt like I was suffocating. Like so many, I was screaming, "I can't breathe!" in a resounding echo. However, for a multitude of reasons, life wasn't playing by my rules or any rules for that matter.

I don't think life has any rules. It just does what it does.

No bias. No reservations. No hesitations. It just completes its task.

It's an understatement to use the phrase "the pressures of life". 2018 was seamless compared to 2019 and 2020. Things were all right and going well. In 2018, I was making plans, goals, and moves to do some amazing things spiritually, physically, and financially. I guess I was making resolutions.

And then BOOM, I'm Loki from the "Puny God" scene in The Avengers film in which he's thrown around by Hulk. Loki is to me as Hulk is to 2019 and 2020. The saying "If you want to make God laugh, tell Him your plans" is true because my plans were unquestionably vanquished. Now, I'm gathering my broken pieces and putting them back them together again as well as I possibly can.

In the Judas of Discomfort chapter, I mentioned the simultaneous deaths that occurred in my family. I understand death is a part of life. However, my family hadn't experienced death often, so when this happened to us, it was unprecedented and without notice. We lost both the patriarch and matriarch in the family on both sides of the family. My family is blessed with longevity. My maternal great-grandmothers lived full lives. One was 97 years old, and the other lived to 101 years old. Both my paternal and maternal grandparents lived to be in their late 80s and early 90s.

I'm not saying that the deaths were the sole struggles. It's also the timing of it all. Just when I thought I was getting some air to breathe a bit, I was hit with another call. From August 2019 to August 2020, I traveled home more than I ever had since moving away a decade ago, and it wasn't planned.

If you've ever lived away from your hometown, then you know the worst phone call you can get is the call that someone has died or is ill in the hospital, and you're unable to extend the physical comfort of a hug or your simple presence to be with your family during that time.

I'm certain everyone can relate as survivors of this pandemic. Denied access to your loved ones. Unable to let them know that you're there for them. It's troubling.

Well, when those calls began, they became my worst fears come true, and with each call, it seemed to get worse. It messed me up mentally. I'm still processing and coping with it.

I'm not sure how others are handling the pandemic, but I must unplug from social media, the news, and society because I found myself down in a funk. I had to be careful because I was falling into a deep, dark hole, unable to figure out how I got there or how to find my way out. It was real. I found myself having a hard time praying. Like I said, I felt defeated.

I was so discouraged about life, I started scaring myself. I didn't want to write. My appetite changed. I wanted to stay in bed all day. Every room in my house started looking like my granddaughter's playroom. The stress of bills, car trouble, work deadlines, trying to keep my MG in check, and still finding time to check on and take care my family were all becoming exhausting. Still, I put on a facade like all was well when it wasn't.

I needed help– and fast.

The Judas of Discouragement will cause you to lose focus. It'll make you stop looking at the everyday blessings you receive and instead have you looking for what has been left behind, lost, or taken away. Focusing on what was rather than what is is like driving a car forward but focusing on what's in the rearview mirror. You're putting emphasis on something that is no more.

Don't misunderstand.

The rearview and side view mirrors serve their own purposes. However, their purposes are not greater than what is ahead. If they were, their sizes would be equal to the windshield you use to see what's ahead.

Sometimes I think we put more blame on God than we'd like to admit. Even more so, we double that blame on the Enemy. However, so little blame is placed on ourselves. I'm not saying every discouragement is self-inflicted. I'm saying that there is always a choice when we're faced with opposition. For every defense, there is an offense. Lingering in discouragement can suck you into a hole that you may not be able to recover from wholly. Discouragement isn't intended to be permanent. In fact, the longer it outstays its welcome, the harder it becomes to push forward when opportunities present themselves.

Have you ever been in a "should've, could've, would've" situation, but because you didn't react in the moment based on a feeling, or you did react in the moment based on the feeling, it caused a chain reaction that you think about often? Maybe the Judas of Discouragement should've stayed three days, but because you wanted others to feel your pain, wrath, or frustration, or you wanted to give someone a piece of your mind, the discouragement turned into three weeks, three months, or three years.

Realize this: you have to stop going around giving people a piece of your mind. That's why you're going crazy. You keep giving your sanity and wisdom away to people who haven't earned it. Your solitude and peace are the most important things you have. Being a light for others is what's important. If people can't handle your greatness, that's not your issue. That's an issue they must take up with God, not you. Therefore, it's all right to go through. It's all right to feel defeated, discouraged, or down in the dumps. However, it's not okay to succumb to those feelings because feelings are fleeting. You don't need to act on something that is meant to be temporary.

Be careful. The Judas of Discouragement can do a whammy on you. Know that you're equipped with the right tools to make it through whatever is placed before you and on you. I know this because, when I felt like I was spiraling out of control and didn't know which end was up or down,

God reminded me that I always come out on top when I activate my faith and decide to face adversity head on and persevere. John 16:33 tells us, "I have told you these things, so that in Me you may have peace. In this world you will have trouble. But take heart! I have overcome the world."[15]

Judas of Disobedience
✝

Ever heard the sayings "Fat meat is greasy?", "A hard head makes a soft behind?", and "A bought lesson is the best lesson"?

Growing up, these were some of the most quoted clichés I heard but turned out to be the greatest teachers in my lifetime. Honestly, I paid for too many lessons that were given to me freely. Some I overpaid. Some I underpaid.

However horrible it is to admit, it's true. I paid for a taught lesson. It was an unnecessary cost I paid because of my actions and decisions. That's because the Judas of Disobedience was all over me during different eras of my life.

Remember when I said I'm not the type to say no? This is that chapter.

When I graduated high school, I remember receiving so many words of wisdom from elders, family, friends, teachers, and even strangers. I have two vivid memories I can recount when I knew I was being disobedient but at the time my spirit wasn't bothered by it.

I'd graduated high school, and I was close to leaving for college. In fact, I believe I was leaving that week. It was the last Sunday I'd attend my church for a while. After service, I was standing in the middle aisle, unengaged with people who were trying to talk with me and wish me well. Because I was unengaged, I just smiled, nodded, shook a few hands, and thought, I'm out of here.

Then, something that seemed to be random happened: a woman I didn't know grabbed my hand. She held it a few moments before speaking to me.

I was confused for two reasons. One– I didn't know this woman. Two– why was she just holding my hand? Being eighteen years old, I thought it was weird. When she started speaking to me, I wasn't listening. I'm not sure if she knew I wasn't listening to her or if it was the spirit telling on me. Either way, she kept repeating herself. That caught my attention.

As a result, I smiled at her and said, "Thank you."

I tried to release my hand from her grip, but she held it tight. Finally, I looked her in the face and said, "Yes, ma'am", hoping that would make her let me go. She didn't.

She looked me right in my eyes and said, "Listen to me, baby. You're about to go on a journey. Your life has an anointing. The Enemy isn't happy because he couldn't destroy you before, so he's on your path strong now. Keep following God. Listen to Him; be careful of those who will try to make you a friend. Keep following God. Listen to Him, and you won't go wrong."

I nodded, smiled, and said, "Yes, ma'am."

She gave me one last look and said, "You hear what I say?"

I nodded again. She released my hand, and I walked away. I could still hear her praying for me as I continued walking towards the exit of the church. I never got her name. I wish I would've. She was nice. Genuine. Kind. Sincere. The least I could've done was get her name. She only wanted what was best for me.

Well, let's just say that that teenager didn't listen to her advice…at first.

I got to school, and I did just enough to get by for a while. I hung out with everybody, even those who didn't have my best interest at heart. Many of them didn't. However, right after midterms, I realized I didn't recognize the girl I'd become. I wasn't persistent or consistent and was only doing enough to get by.

I. Was. A. Slacker. A bum. Ugh! My work was poor quality. My professors were getting the wrong opinions of me. This wasn't how I was raised. I knew right from wrong. I knew how to behave, but I kept doing wrong. Intentionally. Now, since I've given it some serious thought, I know why I was encouraging the Judas of Disobedience. Mostly, it was because I felt like I was carrying the title of "Christian", "goody-two shoes", "bougie", and "stuck up". That was not the association I wanted.

Being a Christian didn't seem cool. Though it conflicted my spirit, I felt the need to rid myself of that identity. Again, I was young and trying to find my way. Although I knew I had a lot going for myself, I didn't understand it at that time. I also didn't understand the size of my destiny. Finally, after I was exhausted from trying to be something I clearly wasn't and doing things that just made me feel like I wasn't living up to my family's name or expectations and frighteningly failing in life, I returned to what I knew. My faith. My teachings. My upbringing. I began a daily bible study. I'd call my mom and discuss certain things in the bible to get a better understanding or to figure something out. I was studying my bible more during my college years than I did the entire time I lived at home. I wanted to build a solid relationship with God, not just to check off something like a religious to-do list. That's what I did. I started a sincere relationship with God. I found myself in a healthier, safer place mentally, physically, and socially because of it.

Another lesson the Judas of Disobedience taught me was just because you don't want a certain reality for yourself, it doesn't mean it's right to try to alter it by acting out. I was in a long-term relationship, but it was toxic for the both of us. Still trying to prove a point to those I felt were in opposition to my desires, I became so disobedient and defiant towards my mom, family, and God. Even when I realized it wasn't what I wanted because it wasn't healthy for either of us, still wanting to prove something, and because I didn't want to be a stereotype or statistic, I stayed in it longer than I should've.

It had gotten to the point that my writing became very dark, depressing, and a bit demeaning. I wasn't thinking clearly. We argued all the time, and I was accepting being belittled, mistreated, and manipulated. Then, those behaviors attached themselves to me, and I started reciprocating those behaviors because I despised feeling defeated. Internally, my attitude was unattractive, but I kept putting up a facade to get through.

Being disobedient was exhausting, and it cost me a great number of things, some of which I can't recover because of my defiance. Some required me to rebuild bridges so I could cross them again. Others are now coming back around so I can complete them effectively. My second chance. Focused on trying to fit in and beat a statistic, I became a clone, trying to be everyone else except who I was made to be. I don't know why I was so unhappy with just being me. When you're a clone, you look and sound the same.

Because I downgraded and entertained disobedience, it cost me...me.

I was unable to say no. My gift became my curse. It still hurts when I think about my acts of disobedience. I want to see people happy, so I often sacrifice myself, and it always ends with me losing what costs the most. Since I kept going along with doing things that I shouldn't have, it caused a lot of my blessings be put on delay. I had to work twice as hard for what would've been given to me freely. I had to earn it and prove myself, not because I wasn't worthy, but because I was mishandling my gift of "no". I was saying it, just to the wrong person. Like I said, I was intentionally doing wrong. Therefore, the person who kept hearing "no" should've been the person to hear "yes".

I have had more than two encounters with the Judas of Disobedience, but those encounters made me who I am today. This Judas still pays me reoccurring visits, but I'm not that young girl anymore. I see, hear, and process things differently. In life, that's how it should be. Grow in and learn from your experiences, especially if you had to pay for the lesson. My gift is no longer my curse. I can and do use my gift of "no", whether it's with my absence or silence.

My mama told me a long time ago, "You don't have to tell people what you're going to do or what you're not going to do. Just do it or don't do it."

It's true because actions are louder than spoken words. I can talk all day, but like we tell children, my actions will pave the path for the greatest and most influential lessons. Ever tried to figure out why children learn faster at a young age? It's because their visual skills develop and process faster than their spoken language. Children learn by mimicry and repetition.

My granddaughter is learning American Sign Language. She's not deaf, but her mother has a degree in American Sign Language and is completing her Bachelor's in interpretation. There fore, before my granddaughter was able to speak words, her mother began introducing her to sign language. Some of my family questioned if this would be confusing for her to learn sign language. However, seeing how my granddaughter has advanced in this language, we didn't view it any differently than a child learning English, Spanish, French, or another language. She'll be bilingual and fluent before she's in kindergarten.

My granddaughter and her mom communicate extensively using sign. These aren't simple words but full sentences. As for the rest of my family including myself, not being fluent in sign language, we communicate with her just fine because she speaks very well. My point is that my granddaughter is learning something because of what she sees. That's why it's always important for us to be careful what we do around children, and even more so, others in general. You never know who is watching you.

The Judas of Disobedience teaches a lot of lessons. Whether you decide to buy those lessons or take the free courses offered by those God places on your path is your choice. However, it's also your choice to decide the limit for what you're willing to pay for the lesson. For me, it cost some relationships, peace, and promotions, and I faced some financial setbacks. That's why I'm adamant about helping those who look to do, be, and get better. If I'm allowed the opportunity to help my neighbor, I will. However, I can't overextend myself to those who aren't willing to put in the work.

Ponder this.

I can be in the position to give you the job you want, but if you don't complete the application or come to the interview, it's not my fault if the job is passed along to someone else. Furthermore, suppose you get the job because you completed the first two steps. It's still not my responsibility to ensure you do your part to keep the job. The Judas of Disobedience will cause you to believe a "tit for tat" spirit is what you need to keep what you have or to get what you want when, in fact, it'll do the opposite. It will cause you to push away people or get passed by because of that attitude.

The Judas of Disobedience is a slippery slope. It will take you farther than you want to go, make you do more than you were willing to do, and make you pay more than you were willing to pay.

That's the trick of it all.

Disobedience will pretend to let you think you're in control. However, when you come to yourself, you'll realize the moment you said no to the wrong person, the facade that all is well will vanish, and the reality you thought you were in will be no more.

Judas of Distraction
†

While writing this book, but prior to this chapter, I suffered a blindside. Essentially, the original narrative for this chapter changed because of that blindside. It seemed this Judas came out of nowhere and wreaked havoc on my family's entire world.

Tragic. Shaken. Catastrophic. Arduous. Direct. Incomprehensible. Leaving behind the residue stain of "why?"

I can't begin to process or fathom how any of what my family has met and is still encountering is a means to an end. When this Judas showed up unannounced, I was praying and heard the sweet voice of the Lord say, "Don't get distracted." At first, I didn't understand what that meant. What was the distraction? Who said

I was distracted? This had nothing to do with my prayer. Why was that the word He chose to give? Why couldn't I get a word of peace, healing, or restoration? The questions kept coming, but the loudest question remained "Why?"

The truth of the matter is this situation interrupted our lives abruptly and without warning. We may never get the answer to that specific question, no matter how desperately we want it.

I resolve that the reason we want to know the "why" is to reason with it.

Ever found yourself trying to rationalize information you've received because it doesn't settle well with your spirit? Therefore, you try to find a "why" in order to justify the information you received to make it all make sense. That's the root of the "why". It's not to help us cope, really, because the answers won't change. The truth isn't altered. The fact stands. While the blemished reality becomes another "new normal", through some ludicrous rationale, we condition our minds to believe if we can just get to the bottom line of it all and make it make sense, then we can accept what we already know. However, that's false. It won't change our feelings about the situation. As I said earlier, it won't change the facts. Instead, it'll slow the process of engaging with and embracing the inevitable feelings we try to suppress with the Judas of Distraction.

Disbelief. Grief. Heartache. Disappointment. Upset. Anger. Frustration. Sadness. Whatever is lingering.

I won't directly talk about the situation because it's still too new for me. I'm overly sensitive even thinking about it, and I'm still trying to process this new truth. My family's still coping. If I'm truthful, I can't bring myself to write about it or connect certain words with others because mentally it becomes permanent, makes it all real, and I'm not ready or mentally stable enough to deal with two Judases yet.

However, about a week ago, I was sitting by myself thinking, and the Spirit came upon me. I can't explain it, but it was a good feeling because I had been feeling abandoned, let down and dejected, even though I knew I wasn't. Nonetheless, it didn't change how my heart felt. My spirit was crushed. Is crushed. But I received a phone call. As I was talking, that's when the Spirit reminded me, "Don't get distracted."

Revelation. I was distracted. I let the Judas of Distraction blindside me, not voluntarily, but I got caught up in the residue of "why?" I found myself drowning out everything else because that residue seemed to stain everything. The memories. Every thought. Even a simple mention of their names. I felt like I was suffocating again. They were facts, but they were the only facts the Judas of Distraction wanted me to highlight and remember. However, I was looking at it all wrong, which is exactly what distraction does.

Hence, I had to refocus– not on the distress, but on the gained reward.

There was nothing I could do to change the outcome of the situation. What was done was done. I can't time travel, though I wish I could. Still, even if I got the answers I was looking for, it wouldn't lessen the blow. The feeling of failure wouldn't just disappear. However, now I'm made aware. Without the distraction, the answer didn't change.

The saying "misery loves company" constantly proves to be true. I'm not saying my family enjoys misery because anyone who knows us knows we are happy and are the life of every party. We enjoy having a great time. It's just that, lately, our frequent family gatherings have been testing.

I often say, "Misery loves company, but happiness does, too, so choose your guest wisely."

I believe this wholeheartedly. It's all about the choice.

Though the Judas of Distraction knocked us out with this one, I'm certain we'll get through this, too. It's a process. I understand why I needed that word instead of a word of peace, healing, or restoration. It's because being blindsided leaves you vulnerable. When you're vulnerable, you're susceptible to attack or harm. My Father needed me to be guarded. My guard was down because of this blindside. My distracting thoughts were greater than my intentional prayers. My praise was fading. In my blindsided grief, I was distracted without knowing and became very susceptible prey.

I want to encourage you. Whatever you might be going through, don't get distracted.

Given the times that we live in right now, we can't be defenseless. Don't become the prey. I'm grateful that even when I was in a dark, low place, I was still being safeguarded by Abba. The prayers of the righteous prevail.[16] James 5 talks about the prayer of faith.[16] I believe even while I felt like I had nothing left to offer and the end was approaching, it was my mustard seed faith that invoked the spirit of God to manifest Himself to me so I would be reassured of the promise.

That's what we have to remember, especially when we are forced to face even the worst nightmares and grim realities and although the Judas of Distraction doesn't play fair and is unjust, it can't sway us from staying focused on the promise. People make choices every day. We may question them, and, in some cases, we may receive an answer we don't like. However, it doesn't change why the person acted, responded, or reacted the way they did. That's not our responsibility. We're only responsible for ourselves, and that includes how we respond, react, and move beyond our blindside– or, as I've named it, the Judas of Distraction.

You can only control you.

You can't control others– their thoughts, feelings, motives, or destiny. That's beyond your control. When you allow the residue stain of "why" to steer you away from your promise and destiny, the distractions cause you to go off-course and become defeated in your own promise. In the words of Mrs. McLemore, my fourth grade teacher, "I know you can hear me, but are you listening?"

Don't let the Judas of Distraction be your failure. Though we get blindsided in life, it doesn't mean we're counted out. It just means our comeback will be greater.

Judas of Destruction
†

I've heard the story of the prodigal son[17] many times. Most of the time, the moral of the story ends the same way. The son comes home, his father forgives him, and all is well.[17] My takeaway of that moral is that no matter how bad things are in your life, you can always come home. In this chapter, I'll talk about the Judas of Destruction using the context of the prodigal son because, at some point in our lives, we've all been that prodigal child. We drifted away. It doesn't matter if it was a physical, spiritual, emotional, social, financial, or mental leave. We left with the intent never to return.

I come from a highly creative family. Singers. Dancers. Actors. Writers. Producers. Athletes. Artists. Each with a special gift to share with others. Whether the gift is productive or counterproductive, the choice is to each his own. It doesn't take away from the gift. Destruction comes in many forms. I'm not tackling all of them in this chapter. However, if you've ever seen the damage destruction does, you know it's a long road ahead when it's time to assess the damage and reconstruct when the dust settles.

One thing about destruction is it doesn't just affect the person being destructive. It destroys all of its surroundings. Destruction, according to Dictionary.com, is "the action or process of causing so much damage to something that it no longer exists or cannot be repaired; a cause of someone's ruin".[18] That's right. The Judas of Destruction will be your ultimate demise if you're not careful enough to get as far away from it as you possibly can.

Let's be real. No one's willing to call himself or herself a "prodigal" because the word means to be wasteful and reckless with resources.[19] The thought of being wasteful, reckless, and inhabiting this sense of destruction at any point of your life is upsetting. Whether the destruction you're doing is intentional or unintentional is irrelevant. What is relevant is being aware of your destruction but not finding the healthy solution to stop it.

In 2009, I was on a serious and destructive path. My home life was in shambles. My friendships were rocky. My health was on a serious downward spiral, and I found myself doing more damage than good to everything that I touched or was connected to me, even when I thought I was helping.

My grandfather would always say, "I am my own worst enemy."

This resonated with me because I couldn't get out of my own way, thinking I was owed something but didn't know what I was owed. I convinced myself I was better than what I was, but I was much worse. I believed I could do it on my own because when I tried to do it through prayer or with help and assistance from friends, family and God, it hadn't gotten me where I wanted to be in the time frame I felt it should or had set forth.

I was the prodigal daughter. Full of myself.

I essentially isolated myself and turned away from what I knew was true, important, and respectable so I could make things happen on my own. Let me be clear: my faith wasn't shattered. My hope wasn't crushed. My love for God wasn't diminished. I was just doing me because of how I was feeling in the moment.

Remember I told you feelings are fleeting?

My choices, based on those fleeting feelings, nearly cost me my family, possessions, and life. I couldn't see past my arrogant, self-righteous ego while truth and life were being spoken into me. I refused to listen and accept truth. If it didn't line up with my agenda, I didn't want any part of it. That's the truth. Again, I'll say that I allowed the Judas of Destruction to use me freely, and it nearly cost me everything.

For years, I was ashamed to think about my actions and the hurt they caused so many in my life. I couldn't fathom the thought that, even in that short period, I allowed my flesh to overrule my spirit and to refute my upbringing. However, I'm grateful and pleased to say that the actions of that girl aren't who God says I am. Since I know who I am in Christ, I hold my head high and walk in authority. I'm no longer held captive to the past. I won't allow anyone else to hold me captive, either, because I'm forgiven.

You may be pondering what caused me to become the prodigal daughter. Well, if we really knew why the prodigal son became the prodigal son, then I could give you the answer. Unfortunately, I don't have it, except for a season or two that God gave me to myself and let me try to do it on my own. I'll be very honest with you. It was hard, embarrassing, shameful, ugly, and– most importantly– lonely. I didn't recognize who'd I become because I'd strayed so far away that trying to find my way back seemed like an escape room, and I couldn't find a way out.

While on my destructive path, I turned people who only meant me well into the villains. I resisted anything that would let me feel like I was important, worthy, or good enough. Truthfully, that was a dark time in my life. I wasn't happy with anything that was going on during that time. I felt like I was a burden to everyone around me. Ultimately, I started doing things I thought would push them away, but it only made them draw closer to me until I forced them away.

In 2009, I was depressed and was involuntarily put into a mental hospital because my drive to live was declining so fast that I couldn't tell one end from the other. The black hole sucked me in, and I couldn't pull myself out. In retrospect, it's scary to know even when your hope and faith is proved in Christ, you can have a Judas that makes you become insecure and volatile to everything around you. To God be the glory because the prayers of the righteous prevailed[16], and I'm here today to tell the story and give a word of inspiration to those who feel they can't be redeemed because of the mistakes they have made. Colossians 1:13-14 says, "For He has rescued us from the dominion of darkness and brought us into the kingdom of the Son He loves, in whom we have redemption, the forgiveness of sins."[20]

Know this. The devil is a liar. Romans 8 declares that nothing can separate us from His love.[21] The beauty in this is it doesn't matter if you're a believer or not because we're all created by the Father. His love for us is also attached to our destiny. I'm grateful to know that, even while going through my destructive phase, He saw fit to have mercy on me, and when I returned home, the celebration was infinite.

I wasn't completely restored, healed, or set free right away, but I could rest in knowing the Judas of Destruction didn't win. Eventually, I found myself again. That bold fireball had returned, and I would fight with every breath to keep her alive and thriving. I had a hard downfall. I fight daily to keep the Judas of Destruction at bay because I remember those tribulations more than I'd like. Though I learned many lessons during that period in my life, it's still hard to face sometimes.

You may have experienced circumstances that you realize were to your own demise. Though they weren't your fondest moments, understand they were allowed because you wouldn't be who you are at this moment in your life if it weren't for your Judas of Destruction. Therefore, smile because even though it is what it is or was, it's not what it's going to be.

Your Judas of Destruction tried it, but it didn't prevail.

Judas of Disgrace
†

I was a Christian, a teenager, and pregnant. I was active in ministry at my home church and thought I was okay because, throughout my entire life, I learned as a Christian that God forgives. However, as an unwed mother, I learned it's a double standard. I was treated as an outcast, and I couldn't understand why. I mean, the dirt I have on so many churchgoers...

It was baffling to me that they'd treat me as if I were the disgrace. Cast out and cast down. However, I'm grateful for that lesson because it made me better and taught me what I was really learning in church was religion.

This chapter isn't about bashing religion, Christians, churches, or anything like that. It's to discuss the hurt and healing brought on by people and relationships. I was hurt, but I was helped, even though at the time it only seemed like a bunch of hypocrites trying to prove a point, be relevant, and keep the facade of their Christian faith intact. I'm not dismissing what I did, but I was judged by a lot of people who hid skeletons in more places than their closets. I've never been one to be popular for speaking falsehoods. I'm the one to speak the truth. The truth is that self-righteous, sacrilegious wannabes will always make you feel inferior and shine the light on others to keep the focus or attention off the true disgraces…themselves.

I trusted someone with my secret at the church. It was someone who I mistakenly considered a friend, but the ultimate betrayal cut me deep. It turned our relationship, and it's never been the same. It's twenty-three years later, and I'm all right with how the situation played out – not because I showed up any of those who brought public shame into my life with the Judas of Disgrace, but because I have literally watched God prepare my table in front of my enemies, and nothing I could've attempted to do in retaliation would have been more fulfilling than watching God be faithful to my family and me.

As I was saying, I was a Christian, a teenager, and pregnant. This was in my junior year of high school when I should've been focused on life after graduation, high school dances, and just being a care-free kid. That wasn't my focus.

It was to graduate, go to college, and do well so my baby would know what it takes to be successful despite the obstacles life throws your way.

No, my baby wasn't an obstacle to me, but the more flack I received from church folks, the harder it became to go to church. I eventually stopped.

I had to step down from ministry because I was told my pregnancy was an indiscretion to the people of God. Catch it. Not to God, but to the people of God. Even though the only thing they'd created was chaos.

They said, "It isn't appropriate. It's not a good look." I confronted the pastor, but I received little aid. The decision of the board stood. That's when it became clear that they quoted the bible but didn't believe it enough to live or practice it.

Who would've thought? The place that's supposed to be a spiritual hospital for those looking for and needing help and healing was aborting more lives than resuscitating them. I was a casualty who didn't even know I'd signed a DNR.

Though I had a lot of support from my family, I also noticed support from somewhere I didn't expect…the world. I was shunned away from the one place I thought would welcome me with open arms in a great time of need and distress, bound and gagged until my "indiscretion" went away post-pregnancy.

Here's one of my strongest dilemmas. The entire time of being raised in the church, all I kept hearing was how much God loved us, how the church was a safe place, how everyone was welcome, "come as you are", and so on.

Then, in a moment of calamity when I needed to cash in on those kind words, compassion, and effort, the check was void. I was holding on to nothing but empty words from people I'd known my entire life. Talk about damaged goods.

My pregnancy caused a revolution at the church. People were split because seeing the damage that it had caused so many times before me was like an uprising. However, by the time they'd figured it out, I was long gone and unbothered by what consolation they'd try to offer me. The Judas of Disgrace had already made its entrance, and, like the domino effect, it was already set in motion. It wasn't until later that I realized I shouldn't have allowed what others thought of me or my situation to decide the relationship I wanted to develop with God. They couldn't make that choice or decision for me. However, I was young in Christ and didn't do as 2 Timothy 2:15 commanded. I let the Judas of Disgrace submerge me. When I discovered who I was, I vowed that my children and everyone I met wouldn't feel what I felt from so many I thought would cover me in prayer yet instead chose to expose me like the adulterous woman. Once I regained my self-confidence and assurance in Him, I knew I wouldn't be taken by the religious vultures again.

It was nearly a decade before I actively took part in ministry again. Pastors and members were changing by the day, but that stigma and foul taste lingered with me for years. Deep down, I think I wanted an apology. Later, I realized the apology wouldn't have changed anything. Changed behavior toward God's people who were coming earnestly, looking for and needing help and healing, and wanting to transform their lives would be the solution. Again, the experience I had with the church, which I thought was a place to help the spiritually sick but turned into a gathering place for many to check off a box showing "task complete", was definitely an eye-opener for me. After much prayer, meditation, and spending time in God's word, I learned more about and for myself than any sermon I'd heard. I was enlightened. After my enlightenment, I shared it with everyone.

I'm not that pregnant teenager anymore. However, the Judas of Disgrace caused my walk with God to grow far beyond my imagination. I embraced the entire experience. It was a teachable moment for me. Though it was uncomfortable and seemed unbearable, I made it through. I wanted to be angry and hold a grudge, but the more I began to draw near to God, the lighter I felt because His spirit encompassed me.

I'm not sure what the Judas of Disgrace has tried to do to make you feel inferior, intimidated, or unworthy. Just know that you're none of those things. Don't let the Judas of Disgrace stay longer than its reservation. Don't allow people to label and stigmatize you with their insecurities. 1 Peter 2:9 declares, "...you are a chosen generation, a royal priesthood, a holy nation, God's special possession..."[22] Therefore, what anyone else thinks is not valid because the only validation you need is given by the I Am.

Now, go forth and reclaim your beauty. Release the dis- and walk in grace.

Judas of Distrust
✝

Ever walked into a room and felt like you were the topic of discussion? It wasn't because you were paranoid. It was for obvious reasons, such as everyone looking at you with the "that's them" look. Maybe when you entered the room, and everyone became awkwardly silent. Or (my favorite) maybe you walked into the room, and there was suddenly this overexcitement to see you and raised pitch in their voices because they were caught off-guard by your sudden appearance.

It's as if an elephant has entered the room, and– newsflash– you're the elephant.

I'm a firm believer that without trust in a relationship, you don't have anything. People closest to me can attest that when my trust is lost, it's hard to earn again. I don't tend to let repeat offenders into my space. This isn't because I lack trust in my own life, am jealous or envious, but it's because I'm incredibly careful with my trust. I often say, "I treat my trust like my money. I don't give it to everybody." You can agree or disagree with me. It's your choice, but it doesn't change the fact that if you're not careful and intuitive to the spirit, you'll find yourself in predicaments that should've, would've, and could've been avoided had you listened to your inner spirit.

Distrust, simply put, is to "regard with doubt or suspicion".[23] It's important you're aware when this Judas is present. It's imperative you're synced with the Spirit. Otherwise, you may miss blessings because you suspect they're curses (and vice versa). The Judas of Distrust is underhanded, problematic, and malicious. It carries a lot baggage and can be difficult to make sense of if you don't know what you're looking for. There will be times when you must make fast decisions and go with your gut feeling to stay or leave. Nevertheless, you shouldn't be eager to jump to conclusions about someone if you haven't given them a fair chance. I said I don't trust easily, but I also don't judge people based on other opinions. Though I continue with caution, I give everyone a fair chance because it's what I want to be given.

I found myself on the receiving end of distrust. It was unnerving because I didn't understand why people would have these preconceived opinions of me. After all, I'm a good person, God-fearing and loving. Why didn't they trust me? Why would they be suspicious of me? Was it jealousy or envy? Later, I learned it wasn't any of those things but instead because of the anointing on my life. My light made it difficult for their spirits to dwell in the same space as me. The Judas of Distrust will rear its wretched head of envy, jealousy, and covetousness to keep others from attaching to you. This isn't a reflection of you, your past, or present. It's about your future because your future is bright. Though you'll feel attacked, unwelcomed, and like you don't belong, stick around because light and darkness can't stay in the same place.

Here's a secret: the light always wins.

In my situation, my relationship with people was a bit uneasy and awkward for a while because it seemed like God was intentional about placing me in certain situations, events, and spaces at the right time to turn the conversation or situation toward Him or just to have a light present to ensure harmony remained intact. Though I didn't always feel comfortable being in the room with specific persons because I knew how they felt about me, I kept being obedient.

Eventually, my light won. Since I remained consistent, which is quite easy if it's your character, I didn't put my integrity in harm's way to prove who I was in order to be accepted by someone who wouldn't be impressed by anything I would do. Seriously, I had already done and carried out so much, and at every turn, it seemed like more fury and resentment kept surfacing. Finally, I had to accept the fact that I'm the person people will either love or hate. There won't be an in-between for me, and I'm okay with that. Therefore, I began to accept the distrust because it's hard to understand someone with strong convictions, especially when they're even harder on themselves about living up to those convictions.

In today's society, you can easily disregard a lot of what people say by observing their actions. People who live by the "I give you my word" creed are few and hard to come by. Therefore, when they come across your path, hold on to them because they are a dying breed. If by chance you are the breed, continue to shine and train up the next generation. Let it be embedded into their DNA. It must be so deeply rooted that when the Judas of Distrust comes around, it becomes troubled, anxious, and apprehensive. Thus, the only choice is forcing distrust to return from whence it came.

Don't compromise or jeopardize your character and integrity. People are watching you– those you least expect and others who have a story to tell. Either way, keep being great and shining bright.

Judas of Discord
†

I'm amazed to hear people talk more about those they don't like than those they claim to love. Is it because secretly we're a drama-driven society? Is it because we like messiness and pettiness?

I guess it's similar to the way that we can know the lyrics to a song we profess to dislike but forget and make up lyrics to our favorite song. Still, I must wonder, is being positive a mere fantasy? Is it just an obscure idea?

Of course not.

It's all about our surroundings, circumstances, and retraining our minds. I've never been the person caught in a lot of drama. In fact, at all costs, I try to avoid it. There's something about confusion that makes me unsettled in my spirit. However, it doesn't mean conflict isn't occasionally lurking around several corners. It does mean I have to be vigilant in prayer to avoid it at all costs.

A couple of years ago, I found myself in an extreme amount of discord. One moment, things were peaceful, cordial, and in sync. In the blink of an eye, the Judas of Discord came to stay. I was confused because I didn't understand the purpose of the discord. If you ever want to see me break down, bring drama to my front door. I'm not talking about mayhem and foolishness. That's different. I'm talking about people being intentionally messy and petty, keeping up friction because for some strange, diabolical, and antagonistic reason, seeing others at odds is an adrenaline rush for them.

Get that away from me.

I don't like it. I don't entertain it.

Again, at all costs, I avoid it and people who keep it up, giving life to it.

Think through this. Messy people are like flies. Flies carry bacteria, viruses, and parasites. Naturally, when you see a fly, you swat it. If a fly lands on your food, do you still eat it or throw it away? Consider the messy people in your life – the gossipers, troublemakers, trouble keepers, liars, thieves, sapsuckers, leeches, and waste carriers that use you as their dumping ground and disposal. They dump their bacteria, viruses, and parasites into your peaceful and harmonious life. They make es. In fact, I was getting completely knocked out, so much so that I'd gotten out of character.

When I say it was bad, it was worse than that.

I recall the day I made up my mind that I wouldn't fall prey or be susceptible to this Judas anymore. I was going about my day as usual, and then someone brought me some negative information. Some "he said, she said".

Again, I was the topic of discussion, the cause of everyone's downfall, and folks were having private meetings about me. I didn't know whether I should be more upset that this discord was still going on or if I should be frazzled because I had to listen to this same tale that kept getting exaggerated, and the person bringing it to me should've let it stay where it was. Weeks had passed, and I considered this issue to be resolved because I went to the person and apologized for anything I did to offend them, and we both agreed it was settled.

I couldn't take it anymore. I snapped.

Those who were around me were speechless.

I'd never done that before. Ever. It was way out of my character. I broke down.

From that day on, I committed to myself that I wouldn't allow anyone to take me to a place like that ever again. I decided if I didn't go there voluntarily, no one else could take me. I didn't care if they told the entire world a fictious rendition of events in their account.

their struggles and strife your struggles and strife.

You are the power of attorney over what you receive spiritually, emotionally, physically, and socially from people. The continued cycle of listening to and entertaining messy people disrupts your feng shui. Thinking "I just let them talk; I don't say anything" is like believing that just because you go to the doctor for the diagnosis but then refuse treatment, you won't receive a bill. Psych! Messy and petty people's thoughts, words, behaviors, and mannerisms are seeping into your soul. Resist the devil, and he will flee.[24]

As I was saying, a couple of years ago, the Judas of Discord was at every corner. I felt as if I were a walking bullseye. It was like I had a target on my back.

I'd been marked, and it was open season on Machael.

I didn't like it. It was upsetting. It had gotten so out of control, it consumed my thoughts and dreams, and my attitude became very sour. I wasn't the Machael others loved and enjoyed being around. I was ready to step down from ministry, leave my job, and write everyone off. I couldn't get a grip on what was happening, let alone process it, leaving me so frustrated because I was trying my hardest to stay positive, be the bigger person, and shine my light for the world to see. However, the Judas of Discord wasn't withholding any punch-

I wasn't concerned about how many people chose to believe the lies being spread about me. I knew that if people chose to believe something that was clearly out of my character, then they weren't who I thought, anyway, and I didn't need to entertain them or keep them as company. It wasn't worth my time, energy, or peace.

The Judas of Discord's days of coming to conquer and divide had finally come to an end. I had to make the conscious decision to release it and all its counterparts, including the Judas of Dysfunction, Judas of Disappointment, and Judas of Disturbance. I'd take the stand to move forward. This meant leaving others behind because I didn't want to become bitter and angry, especially toward my family because they were the ones catching the fury of Machael every time some new drama came up. I'd had enough.

Please listen. People will try to villainize you because you are cut from a different cloth. They'll intentionally make you feel like you're the one doing wrong, being disruptive, and causing discord. However, I've learned that when the Enemy knows your purpose is to help bring peace and push people to their destiny, he'll do anything to keep it from manifesting and coming to fruition.

I am telling you- don't back down from your purpose. Keep doing what's right. Continue to rise above the situation. Stay the course, and, as my big sister says, "provoke positivity". With everything else going on in the world, there's enough negativity, pessimism, and discord. Avoid people who only look to sow discord. This world needs a little more love.

Be encouraged and know this Judas has an agenda. It's to bring you out of character. It's to isolate and ostracize you. It's to make you feel inferior so you won't think you're adequate enough to help bring others into the light and harmony.

Stand firm. You're a natural-born leader, called to do world-changing things.

Judas of Difficulty and Distress

†

When we're constantly told that misery loves company but not reinforcing that happiness does, too, there's a problem. When we're being told, "You are what you eat" but not "You are what you speak", there's a problem.

Are we suggesting we should encourage people to speak death and not life? They should speak debt and illness instead of wealth and good health? Are we suggesting people should speak defeat and survival instead of overcoming and thriving? Is speaking suffering and strife the way to go?

Absolutely not. In fact, it is the opposite.

We should speak victory because we are a victorious people. If you've been living long enough, you can testify that tests and trials come with this thing called life. Though some tests and trials may be a bit more difficult than others, the lasting effects they have on a person are permanent. However, it's our outlook that must be considered.

I'm going to use the analogy of a pop quiz versus a final exam to explain this chapter. While both are tests, they are vastly different. Unlike the final exam, the pop quiz is more frequent, unexpected, and doesn't carry as many points as the final exam. However, that doesn't take away from its purpose and result. While the final exam is expected, limited to a specific time, and carries a lot of weight, its purpose and result are only determined by the preparations leading to the final exam, including the pop quizzes, performance, and participation in class.

When I was studying for my undergraduate degree, I remember receiving so many syllabi from my professors, it seemed to be overwhelming. However, the syllabus was to prepare me for the expected. A few of my professors on occasion would have a surprise waiting for the class when we arrived. They'd throw us a curve ball. At the time, it was very frustrating because I'd come to prepare myself for what was on the syllabus. I couldn't understand why they would go through all the trouble to create and distribute a syllabus if they were going to deviate from the plan. Although I didn't realize it at the time, looking back at it now, the truth is that I was being shaped, molded, and prepared for things known to those older and wiser than me.

It's called the unexpected. While I couldn't appreciate these uncertainties at the time, I'm incredibly grateful for them now because they taught me more than I'd realized in the moment.

Now, I used the terms "pop quiz" and "final exam" because they're relatable to anyone who has been a student. Ever been minding your business, and, what seems like out of nowhere, something just happens? You're unprepared, you haven't studied for it, and, in fact, you're trying to play catch up because you've fallen behind. This is the pop quiz technique.

In the other scenario, you're studying for something you know is coming and doing everything to prepare. This is the final exam technique.

While both techniques are tests in theory, they are much more than that. It's the arrival and the approach of handling life battles and wars that make the difference. This leads me to my last discussion of a Judas in this book, which is the Judas of Difficulty and Distress. Proper handling of your tests and trials is vital to what you learn while going through them and how to overcome. Without that, you'll find yourself on repeat, and it will become even harder and frustrating, causing you to fail before you can even get started. This will happen because you won't be in the right mindset to win what was already declared as a victory for you.

Pop quizzes can be nerve-wracking for students. This is because the quizzes aren't planned, and, to some students, they seem pointless and counterproductive. To these students, they seem this way because they haven't figured out the purpose of a pop quiz. When considering a pop quiz at face value, it can seem counterproductive or pointless. However, when you go beyond the superficial and trivial exterior of something, you'll come to appreciate its real value and all it has to offer.

Final exams are stressful for any student because, depending on the professor, the test may be comprised of many different things, so you find yourself trying to study everything. Then, on the day of the test, the one thing you didn't study is on the test. Instead of focusing on the information you know, you lose focus and zone in on everything you don't know. Most likely, it's something simple and minute.

Listen to me. It's a trick.

Do not consume yourself with the unknown. You know much more than you give yourself credit for, and you must use it to your advantage and not allow it to be your defeat or ruin.

The Judas of Difficulty and Distress will cause you to refocus on the unknown and uncertainty because when we're in places like that, it's scary. Ever watched a child trying to walk for the first time? Their instinct is to reach or grab for something because taking a step forward without knowing what is to come next is frightening. It's the same thing in our tests and trials. Though we're in uncomfortable places and are forced to deal with or face situations that are unpleasant, it doesn't mean they're unnecessary. On the contrary, the Judas of Difficulty and Distress makes us level up and rise to the occasion.

Whether it's a pop quiz or final exam isn't pertinent. The importance and purpose behind the pop quiz or final exam matter. It's the arrival and approach. I had to learn many lessons the hard way. One thing I remember my grandmother taught me was "You must pick and choose your battles. Otherwise, you'll find yourself always in a war." I didn't understand it at the time, but now I have so much clarity. H. Jackson Brown said it like this: "Be willing to lose a battle in order to win the war."[25] Both statements hold value and are true. When going through any test or trial, the only person who can ensure a great result is you. Whether the test or trial is a pop quiz (unexpected) or final exam (anticipated), the arrival and the approach you choose will determine if you only want to win the current battle or save your energy to win the war.

Judas to be Revealed
†

We must understand that fear can bring about something that we never knew existed in us. Look at Adam and Eve. After their act of disobedience, the spirit of fear came upon them.[26] This caused a domino effect for all humankind. This was something God never meant for us to have. He understood we weren't emotionally mature enough to handle the knowledge that dwelled in the garden. Instead of the knowledge being freeing and liberating for us, it became our burden.

I can't fathom what life would be like if the first sin hadn't been committed. However, I understand that since the beginning of time, there has always been a structure set forth, and it includes having a consequence for our actions. While I can't say with a pure heart that I'm delighted with the events happening in the world today, I understand that they don't fall solely on the shoulders of Judas.

We each have a little bit of Judas in us, and we must own it.

Still, it's important to understand the purpose he had to fulfill, just like your life's trials and ups and downs. No one's perfect. No one's exempt. If I'm honest, there are times when I feel like there won't be an ending to the strife, heartache, disappointment, disapproval, and all the other unpleasantries that come with this thing called life, at least on this side.

With the year I've had, it's been hard to hold on to the positive things God has graciously and freely given me…including life itself. I'd be telling a lie if I said that I'm not human and not struggling to stay optimistic. Each day gets a little harder. However, with the hand I've been dealt, I've come to grips with Colossians 3:2, as it says, "Set your mind on things above, not on earthly things."[27] I must do this consistently because when I don't, my spirit isn't well.

Though we don't know what the future holds, and the times we're living in right now are uncertain, I want to impress upon you to live every day as your fresh start, a new beginning, because tomorrow isn't promised to any of us.

This book was birthed from life experiences. Though it was uncomfortable, painful, and heartbreaking for me to talk about, a lot was revealed to me through the journey. Some things are still being revealed to me because I'm learning how to process through this reset. I understand the reset will help me remove any complacencies that keep me from reaching my full potential. As tough as it may be, it's not in vain.

I'll continue to hold on until the lesson is learned and I'm released from the storm. Until that time comes, I'll just watch and wait for the next Judas to be revealed.

References

1 https://www.prayerrelay.com/the-purpose-of-your-judas/
2 Luke 22 (NIV)
3 Matthew 27 (NIV)
4 Matthew 10 (NIV)
5 Matthew 26 (NIV)
6 Luke 9 (NIV)
7 John 12 (NIV)
8 https://www.lyricsmode.com/lyrics/j/james_cleveland/this_too_will_pass.html
9 John 13:27 (NIV)
10 John 18:10-11 (NIV)
11 https://www.umcdiscipleship.org/resources/history-of-hymns-if-it-had-not-been-for-the-lord
12 Galatians 5:22-23 (NIV)
13 https://www.dictionary.com/browse/self-care
14 https://www.ucsfhealth.org/conditions/pregnancy/trimesters
15 John 16:33 (NIV)
16 James 5 (NIV)
17 Luke 15 (NIV)
18 https://www.dictionary.com/browse/destruction
19 https://www.dictionary.com/browse/prodigal
20 Colossians 1:13-14 (NIV)
21 Romans 8 (NIV)
22 1 Peter 2:9 (NIV)
23 https://www.dictionary.com/browse/distrust
24 James 4:7 (NIV)
25 https://www.azquotes.com/quote/768310
26 Genesis 3 (NIV)
27 Colossians 3:2 (NIV)

About the Author

Machael LaShaunda discovered her passion for writing in middle school. She continued nurturing her craft throughout high school and college writing poems, short stories, plays, attending and leading writing workshops. At Lincoln University in Jefferson City, Missouri she studied Journalism and became a member of Sigma Gamma Rho Sorority, Inc. She transferred to the University of Central Missouri in Warrensburg and received her Bachelor of Science degree in Journalism with a minor in Creative Writing.

The family-oriented author is a native of Saint Louis, Missouri born to the late Rev. Albert Borders Sr. and Mrs. Angela Borders. She is the honored wife and mother moved to Little Rock, Arkansas in 2010 with her supportive husband, two magnificent daughters, and Toy Poodle. In 2017, Machael became the proud YaYa of a beautiful granddaughter. She is the youngest of eight children and proud Titi to a host of nieces, nephews, great nieces, and great nephews.

She is a faith believer and active member of Second Baptist Church in Little Rock, Arkansas. As a humanitarian for more than a decade, Machael is genuinely engaged with community outreach, serving homeless and displaced families through partnerships with various local and national nonprofit organizations.

*Our Motto
"Transforming Life Stories"*

Publish Your Book With Us

Our All-Inclusive Self-Publishing Packages
100% Royalties
Professional Proofreading & Editing
Interior Design & Cover Design
Self-Publishing Tutorial & More

For Manuscript Submission or other inquiries:
www.jkenkadepublishing.com
(501) 482-JKEN

Also Available from J. Kenkade Publishing

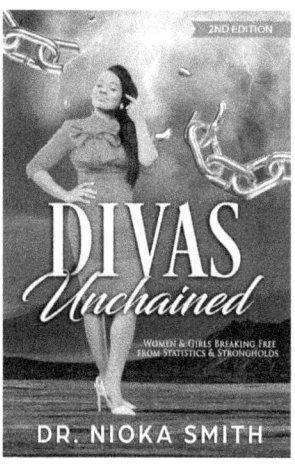

ISBN: 978-1-944486-25-9
Visit www.drniokasmith.com
Author: Dr. Nioka Smith

Sexually abused by her father at the age of 14, pregnant at the age of 17, and a nervous breakdown at the age of 28, Dr. Nioka Smith's painful past almost killed her, until the voice of the Lord guided her into destroying strongholds and reversing Satan's plan for her life. DIVAS Unchained is the powerful chain-breaking reality of the many unfortunate strongholds our women and girls face. Dr. Nioka uses her divine gift to help women and girls break free from destructive life cycles and prosper in all areas of life. Satan has lied to you. It's time to expose his lies. It's time to break free!

Also Available from J. Kenkade Publishing

ISBN: 978-1-944486-83-9
Visit www.amazon.com
Author: Apostle C.A. Turner

There's such a hunger for the things of the spirit and the supernatural. Many have decided to tap into the dark side in order to understand more about the Supernatural and the things of the spirit. One of the reasons for this I believe, is because the church as a whole has lost the desire to see a move of God validated by his power with miracles, signs, and wonders. It's my desire and prayer that this information will activate you in ways you never dreamed as you apply it to your spiritual life.

Also Available from J. Kenkade Publishing

ISBN: 978-1-944486-51-8
Visit www.amazon.com
Author: Jerry Walker

Jerry Walker is an Ambassador for the Kingdom of God, Author, Teacher & Empowerment Speaker. He delivers the word of God with authority, effectiveness, clarity and eloquence. Ambassador Walker shares with his audience that they are fearfully and wonderfully made, without defect, only inaccurate thought processes. Walker is a thought leader ushering in God's presence for the next generation, giving them Kingdom context for a life well-lived. His ministry goes beyond the church building, into the education system, political system and medical system to name a few. Walker continues his ministry at home as he serves his wife and their three children, fulfilling 1 Corinthians 13:4-7.

Also Available from J. Kenkade Publishing

ISBN: 978-1-944486-65-5
Visit www.amazon.com
Author: Ramona Freeman

"Prayer: My Incense to God" is a composition of prayers created by the author over the years for various topics. The purpose of this prayer manual is to set a foundation of prayer and intercession according to the Word of God, to establish prayer in every home, city, state, and nation, and to pray the will of God in order to see His kingdom come on Earth as it is in Heaven (Matthew 6:10).

www.ingramcontent.com/pod-product-compliance
Lightning Source LLC
Chambersburg PA
CBHW051347040426
42453CB00007B/452